A Way with Words

Gary F. Woodson

Inspirational Poetry for the journey of life

COAL UNDER PRESSURE | DAVENPORT

COAL UNDER PRESSURE PUBLICATIONS

A Division of Coal Under Pressure, LLC
109 Ambersweet Way, Suite 280
Davenport, FL 33897

WWW.COALUNDERPRESSURE.COM

Printed in the United States of America

Credit/Copyright Attribution: "Ruslan Ivantsov/Shutterstock Image ID 415666189"

Credit/Copyright Attribution: "Alexander Image/Shutterstock ID 166179467"

Library of Congress Control Number: 2016936342

ISBN: 978-0-9913704-8-1

DEDICATION

This book is dedicated to my father (the late Edgar P. Woodson) who as a published author himself, gave me inspirational footsteps to follow in.

To my mother, Mildred F. Woodson, for constantly reminding me to be grateful and to stay focused on the things that are really important in life.

To my wife, Rose, who supports and encourages me at all times and in all ways, as no one else can.

Contents

Acknowledgements

I thank God for blessing me with the gift and talent of inspirational writing. God was, is, and always will be the guiding force for me on my path as a writer.

To all my family and friends:

Thank You for the love and support you have always shown me. You mean more to me than words can ever say.

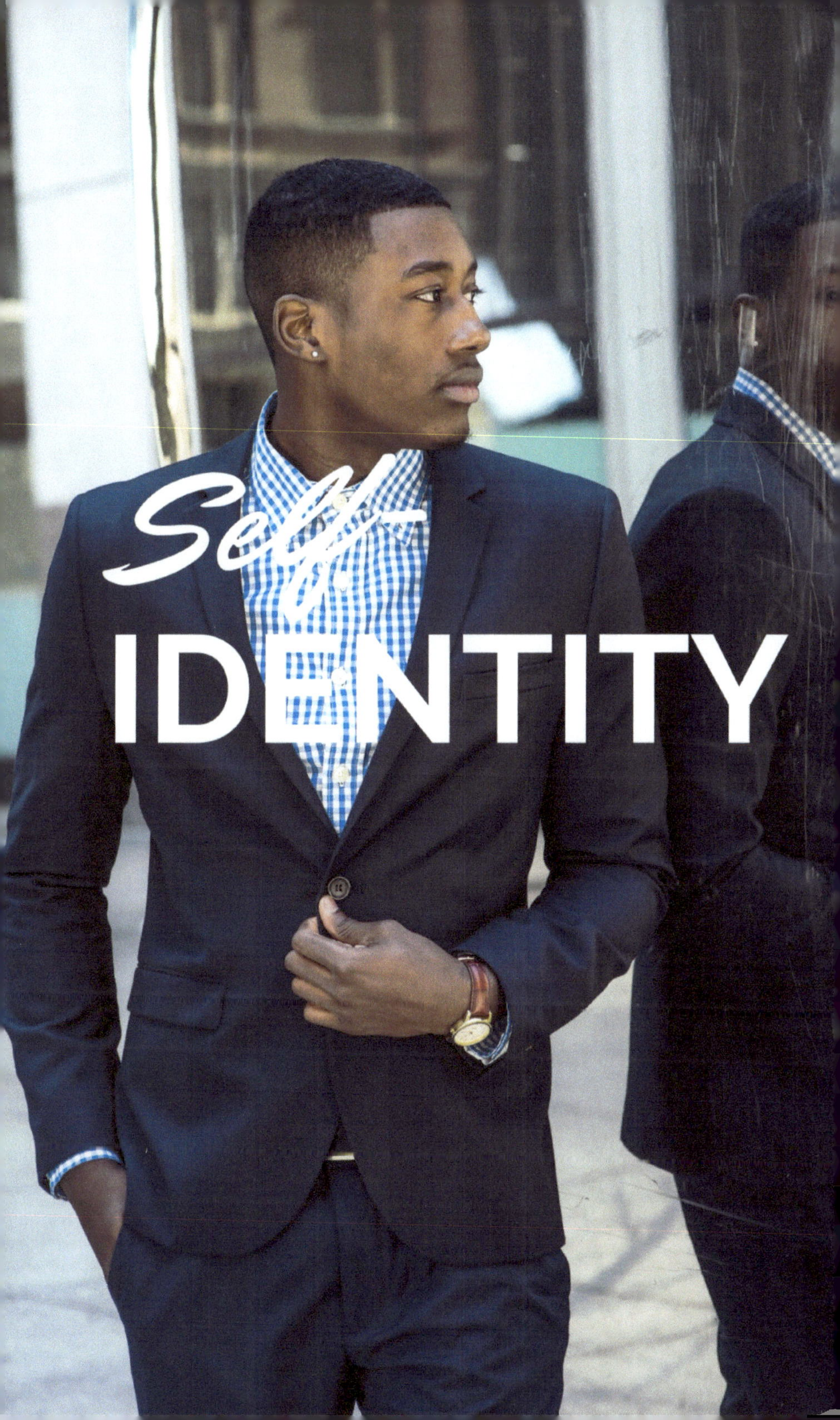
Self-
IDENTITY

BRIDGING THE GAP

I'm the bridge someone will cross,
and somewhere they will go,
so I must always be aware
I play a special role.

It may be a stranger, or a friend
just looking for a smile,
or a child who only wants to play
because it's been awhile.

Bridges can be many things
they always fill a gap,
with outstretched arms, I will meet
someone where they're at.

Someone was a bridge for me,
so let me do the same.
It's down the road we come and go
across the bridge we came.

DON'T FIT IN A BOX

There is no box that I fit in,
I cannot be contained.
There's more to me than meets the eye,
as I forever change.

There is no profile that I fit,
no label that I wear.
Don't look for me to just blend in,
you will not find me there.

I must be free, I must express
who it is I am.
I'll have no part of any box,
controlled by any man.

There is no box that I fit in,
and there will never be.
By myself, I stand alone
unique, because I'm me.

I AM STRONG ENOUGH

When I find I'm tempted to close my eyes,
as life gets really tough...
I'll keep them open and stay strong
and in God I will trust.

For there's only so much that I can see
or I can understand,
but I believe no matter what
the faith on which I stand.

Instead of choosing to run away,
I choose to persevere!
And when I'm scared I won't back down,
but overcome my fear.

When I find I'm tempted to close my eyes,
as things get kind of rough...
I'll keep them open, no matter what,
for, I am strong enough.

IT'S NOT PICTURE PERFECT

Picture perfect it is not,
and it will never be.
The life I know and the life I live
that does belong to me.

I'll make the most of what I have,
and love the life that's mine.
I'll walk in the shoes that are on my feet
by God's will and design.

For no man has a perfect life,
we all have joy and pain.
When the rose colored glasses are taken off
then that is what remains.

Picture perfect it is not,
that is plain to see...
an authentic, honest, life that's real...
the way it's meant to be.

NO GIVING IN, NO GIVING UP

I cannot be somebody else,
pretending that it's me.
I like the person that I am,
it's who I want to be.

Some will like me, some will not
that's just the way it is.
I will not change the way I am,
or change the way I live.

Pleasing others and not myself
would be a big mistake.
I won't give in no matter what.
I will not be a fake.

I'm proud of who and what I am.
I'm different and unique.
To be at peace with who I am
is all I really need.

RE-INVENTING MYSELF

I'm reinventing who I am,
to serve me where I'm at,
for I must change no matter what
the plain and simple fact

The mental clothes I use to wear
don't fit me anymore.
They just no longer meet my needs,
and that I know for sure.

The landscape that surrounds me now,
I survey and do find..........
It's time for me to be transformed
renewed within my mind.

I'm re-inventing who I am,
embracing what must change
adapting to where I find myself,
allowing growth to reign.

REVOLVING REFLECTION

Further along than perhaps I know,
the place where that I am......
is it where I thought that I would be
and is it what I planned?

At any point and time in life
the only thing I know...
is life's a journey that I'm on
no matter where I go.

There's much that I don't understand,
but still I must reflect...
on where I've been and where I am
to see how I am blessed.

What lies ahead will always be
the land of hopes and dreams...
the place I was, the place I am
the place I'll always be.

THE STORY OF MY LIFE

The greatest thing I have to share...
the story of my life.
It's who I am and how I live,
in that which I delight.

From birth to death and in between
in work and while at play...
I'm writing the story of my life
for I have numbered days.

It's all about giving myself away,
I freely choose to share
with family, friends, and others too,
I love and show I care.

For in the end when I am gone,
what I will leave behind...
is the message that my story told,
the way that God designed.

TO BE CONTINUED

Wherever I am at any point
is simply passing through......
not staying long I've much to do,
and must stay on the move.

In the very course of life that is,
beyond what I can see...
I'm moving toward what is unknown
the way it beckons me.

The beginning, middle, and the end...
they all are intertwined.
I live within them, all at once
life's clock keeps track of time.

To be continued is where I live,
the story of my life...
suspense and mystery are my best friends
and they're my guiding light.

WALKING ON

I'm choosing to keep walking on,
because I can't go back.
With planted feet I take each step.
I can't stay where I'm at.

When I fall down I get back up.
I have no time to waste.
I've places to go, things to do,
and so much that's at stake.

By walking with faith and not by sight
whatever is ahead...
is part of the journey I accept
and is the life I live.

I'm choosing to keep walking on,
believing I will find...
the further I go, the more I learn
about this walk of mine.

WHO I'M MEANT TO BE

Giving up who I am right now
for what I've yet to be,
"goodbye" to this and "hello" to that
in order to receive.

There's so much more that I can be,
if I leave status quo...
dreams fulfilled and goals achieved,
when stretched then I will grow.

It's just outside the comfort zone
a path awaits my feet...
the trail that I am meant to blaze
the destiny I seek.

It's believing there is more for me,
and then I have to act
to reach the place I'm going to
I'm leaving where I'm at.

Food for
THOUGHT

I EXPECT THE UNEXPECTED

I expect the unexpected,
so I never am surprised.
When something happens I didn't plan,
I take it all in stride.

Although I would like to really know
the way that things will go,
I have no magic crystal ball.
I just go with the flow.

For life is changing all the time,
and that will always be.
Suspense and mystery fill my life,
and are a part of me.

I expect the unexpected,
include it in my plans.
No matter what this life may bring
surprised I never am!

A DIAMOND IN THE ROUGH

A diamond in the rough I am,
a diamond you are too.
I am the light in someone's life
the same is true of you.

Nuggets of gold and gems of truth,
in someone else we find...
The hope we need to fan the flames
is yours and also mine.

The key is to always shine the light,
to help each other see...
The good that lives inside of you,
the good inside of me.

Just as I am, just as you are
we are what someone needs...
such precious diamonds in the rough
for someone to receive.

A LITTLE ACT OF KINDNESS

Just one little act of kindness,
and random from the heart....
changes the course of all involved,
because you played a part.

We all need to be reminded
while going on our way...
we meet the needs that people have
by what we do and say.

Yes, someone needs the smile you have,
while someone needs your ear.
Be conscious of the little things,
and you will surely hear.

Just one little act of kindness
has power undefined.
The life affected by these acts
is yours and also mine.

DOORS

There are many doors I come across,
once opened I will find...
for better or worse what does await
is on the other side.

Doors get opened all the time,
it's wise to first discern...
is there potential regret that I can see,
or truth for me to learn?

Some doors are meant to be kept closed-
they lead to an empty room,
while others lead to growth and change
where I can be renewed.

The door I choose to open up
can't be a random act,
for once the handle has been turned
it changes where I'm at.

JOY

Happiness is wonderful,
but joy is something more.
Happiness is living,
joy knows what it's for.

Happiness is one thing,
but joy is something else.
Happiness is money,
but joy is having wealth.

Happiness is fleeting,
but joy is here to stay.
Happiness is special times,
but joy is every day.

Joy is found within the soul.
It's something you can't see.
I would rather have joy than be happy,
for joy will never leave.

LIFE ASSIGNMENTS

We do not know how long we have
to accomplish any task.
God assigns us work to do
no matter where we're at.

Given a job and a role to play
a mission to complete,
and when it's time for moving on
it's always bittersweet.

A beginning and completion date
that God alone ordains,
a timeline the human eye can't see
is constant and remains.

Assignments come and they will go,
and when the work is done....
Without regret I can move on
accepting what's to come.

PATIENCE

I must be patient with myself,
and other people too...
for we are all at different points
as through this life we move.

I may go fast, you may go slow.
We each have our own pace.
While traveling on this road of life
we're all in need of grace.

We're quick to judge and slow to care.
We fail to understand...
what it's like to walk in another man's shoes
who needs a helping hand.

So, patient let me learn to be
that I in turn may find...
other people helping me to see
how patience is defined.

QUESTIONS

My life is filled with questions.
There's things I want to know.
This longing just won't go away.
It's coming from my soul.

The search for truth and meaning,
so that I can discern...
whatever life is teaching me
is what I need to learn.

It is a quest that I am on,
to learn all that I can.
Knowledge helps to quench my thirst
to better understand.

Questions big and small exist,
as long as I'm alive...
If there's something I can figure out
then I am asking why.

THE PROCESS OF NAVIGATION

Throughout the course of daily life
I navigate my way,
thinking and acting that reflects
the faith that I obey.

Forks in the road are everywhere,
so which way do I go?
The internal compass that I have
will always let me know.

For choices big and small I make
do impact what will be....
affecting how I look at things,
the eyes through which I see.

Thinking thoughts is connecting dots,
step one and then step two...
getting where I'm trying to go
by navigating through.

WORD ATTRACTION

Words and thoughts are what I have,
and they are mine to use.
For as I think, then so it is
the action that I choose.

Words have power and carry weight.
They hold that special key...
that opens or closes every door,
that leads to what will be.

Like a magnet with forces to attract,
words will bring about...
confidence and strength in who I am,
or fear, despair, and doubt.

When thoughts turn into words we say,
something has to change...
positive or negative I decide
and that is what will reign.

PATH'S THAT CROSS

Paths that cross are not by chance,
some things are meant to be....
for as we try to find our way
alone we cannot see.

So, people come into our lives
at just the perfect time.
The lessons we learn and wisdom we gain
create the life we find.

We never know just where or when
these crossings will take place.
This part of life is a mystery
that destiny must shape.

Along the journey of our lives
some points will intersect.
For, through each life a story's told
with each and every step.

HIGHER GROUND

Higher ground on which to stand
is where my feet belong...
the place where I can clearly see
what's really going on.

With the limited scope of human eyes
I can only see so much,
and for what I'm trying to understand
that is never quite enough.

It's only when the picture's crystal clear
that I can truly see...
the lessons I am being taught
to make a better me.

Higher ground must be my goal
to thrive and be at peace...
I give my thoughts and prayers to God
and higher ground my feet!

www.ingramcontent.com/pod-product-compliance
Lightning Source LLC
Chambersburg PA
CBHW041818040426

42452CB00001B/9

* 9 780099 137048 1 *